The Complete Guide to

Architectural

Carving

by Kurt Koch

Fox
Chapel Publishing Co. Inc.

1970 Broad Street • East Petersburg, PA 17520 • www.foxchapelpublishing.com

Acknowledgments

Special thanks go to Duane Mendenhall of Lancaster, Pennsylvania (www.mendenhallwoodcarving.com) for his generous contribution of time, knowledge and photographs.

The Complete Guide to Architectural Carving is a completely revised and updated combination of Ornamente schnitzen, Teil 1 (Heft 18) and Ornamente schnitzen, Teil 2 (Heft 19), first published in 1998 Kurt Koch. The patterns contained herein are copyrighted by the author. Artists may make up to three photocopies of each individual pattern for personal use. The patterns, themselves, however, are not to be duplicated for resale or distribution under any circumstances. This is a violation of copyright law.

Publisher	Alan Giagnocavo
Book Editor	Ayleen Stellhorn
Cover Design	David Marty
Desktop Specialist	Linda Eberly

ISBN 1–56523–193–7
Library of Congress Preassigned Card Number: 2003107297

To order your copy of this book,
please send check or money order
for the cover price plus $3.50 shipping to:
Fox Chapel Publishing Company, Inc.
Book Orders
1970 Broad St.
East Petersburg, PA 17520

Or visit us on the web at *www.foxchapelpublishing.com*

Printed in China
10 9 8 7 6 5 4 3 2 1

Table of Contents

Getting Started

What is ornamental, or architectural, carving?

Ornamental carvings, or architectural carvings as they are also called, by rule, are always incorporated into an overall design. They can include motives of common natural objects, such as animals or plants. Often they are stylized or fanciful modifications. An example is the classic acanthus leaf motif.

Ornaments are rarely artistically independent works. We see them better as parts of functional objects, such as chairs, wardrobes, mirrors, watches, clocks, columns, books, doors, walls and so on. They are decorations and add incredible beauty to the common objects of our daily life.

Architectural carvings can be used to enhance many types of furniture, including desks, chests of drawers, tables and chairs. This built-in corner cupboard features a large, concave, carved shell. (Carving by Duane Mendenhall, Lancaster, Pennsylvania.)

Ornaments as part of a functional object should elevate and enhance that object's functionality by adding an artistic flair that flows out of the object, imparting a feeling of movement or life from the item. Each ornament generally contains many diversified elements that change and undulate into new and surprising perspectives, giving the impression of multi-dimensionality.

An object may be high in its quality because of the wood used and because of the workmanship employed, but may not catch the eye. A plain wall, ceiling, door, shutter or banister can be brought to life by the addition of an ornamental carving.

What will I learn from this book?

In this edition I offer general learning aids and exercises to quickly develop your ornamental carving skills. Page by page you will learn to carve seven different ornaments—from a simple swoosh to an elaborate flower banner. My advice to you is: Don't carve each project one time only. Instead, carve each at least several times. Repetition of the carving projects presented here will help you to develop a flowing form and exceptional skill.

The projects in this book are geared toward the intermediate and advanced carvers who already possess basic gouge and chisel carving skills but consider themselves beginners in the field of ornamental carving. Ornamental carving is a demanding field in the fine craft of carving. It will never be just another style or method of presenting carvings. As such, you need a firm grounding in the basic techniques before you begin to work through the ornament projects presented here.

All of the ornaments in this book are carved from full wooden blocks. This method of work will also predominate in professional practice. It occasionally happens that the ornaments or decorations are carved separately and then applied to the selected object, but that method is not addressed in this book.

The patterns are copied directly onto the wood and systematically carved out. All of the ornaments have a background, which means that the ornament appears to grow out of this background. In practice this so-called background, or base, can also be convex or concave. The final use of the ornament defines the form of the background.

What kinds of tools are used?

The movement or life brought to most ornamental carvings consists largely of convex and concave forms. Many concave forms can be achieved with conventional gouges (straight shaft with a hollowed edge form). Most can be achieved with gouges having a curved shaft and hollowed edge form, but the addition of back-bent gouges for special situations should allow you to achieve all concave forms.

A perfect technical carving of ornamentation requires an array of specialized and a few common

The techniques of architectural carving can be applied to newel posts at the top or bottom of a flight of stairs. Note the carved features adorning the lower portion of these newel posts. (Carving by Duane Mendenhall, Lancaster, Pennsylvania.)

tools. Every tool, however, must be of the best quality that the carver can afford. Low quality tools can make the process of carving an ornament into a heavy, difficult or impossible task. Using poorly made and formed tools may cause some carvers to wrongly doubt their ability to achieve good results in their carvings. These tool substitutions produce unacceptable cuts and pricks causing a loss of elegance in the total presentation.

An ornament carver must frequently change back and forth among specialized carving tools. Sometimes, cutting a large and concave form can require a different tool with a different profile every five millimeters or so. Switching tools frequently like this will help to avoid visible cutting borders.

The convex form does not require perfectly matched profiles. In these cases you can cut thinner and thinner shavings until the individual cuts, or facets, are no longer visible. The end result is a polished surface.

Check with your favorite woodcarving supply shop to research the wide variety of sophisticated tools that are available for ornament carvers. The gouge chart on page 4 is provided for the comparison of tool edges.

How do I get that smooth look on a finished ornament?

Sanding is an unacceptable practice for the ornament carver. Because of technical reasons, a sanded wooden surface always appears rough. The cut from a perfectly sharpened tool edge is always the best way to build up an ornamental element. This method always results in a brilliant presentation—a pleasure for every eye. No other method will result in the same brilliance as the natural beauty of a cleanly cut surface sculpted with quality, professional, perfectly sharpened and adapted tools.

How do harmony, rhythm and melody apply?

What have these to do with ornamental carvings? In the same way that these three basic elements are necessary for music to be pleasurable to the ears, the eyes accept a well-done ornament as a pleasure when harmony, rhythm and melody are represented and respected in a carving.

The motif must be in harmony with other motifs and with the object upon which it is carved. Do not bring together strange elements as they do not harmonize.

Each motif must have a certain rhythm, a fluid character. Elements that break the flow of the design do not have a place in the complete presentation.

When a motif adheres to the rules of movement, then with a little bit of fantasy, you, the carver, can perceive something like a melody in your carving. There is no interference in the composition, no note out of tune, no displeasure, and you feel a complete satisfaction. If the observer of the ornamental work can feel this optical melody as well—and feel it with pleasure—then the work is well done.

With all that said, let's start with the exercises.

An oak leaf motif is carved into the center plate and end plates of a fireplace mantel. The plates will be glued to the final mantel. (Carving by Duane Mendenhall, Lancaster, Pennsylvania.)

Architectural carving is most often associated with fireplace mantels and entranceways. The mantels on these dual fireplaces feature carved bracelets, a carved egg and dart molding. (Carving by Duane Mendenhall, Lancaster, Pennsylvania.)

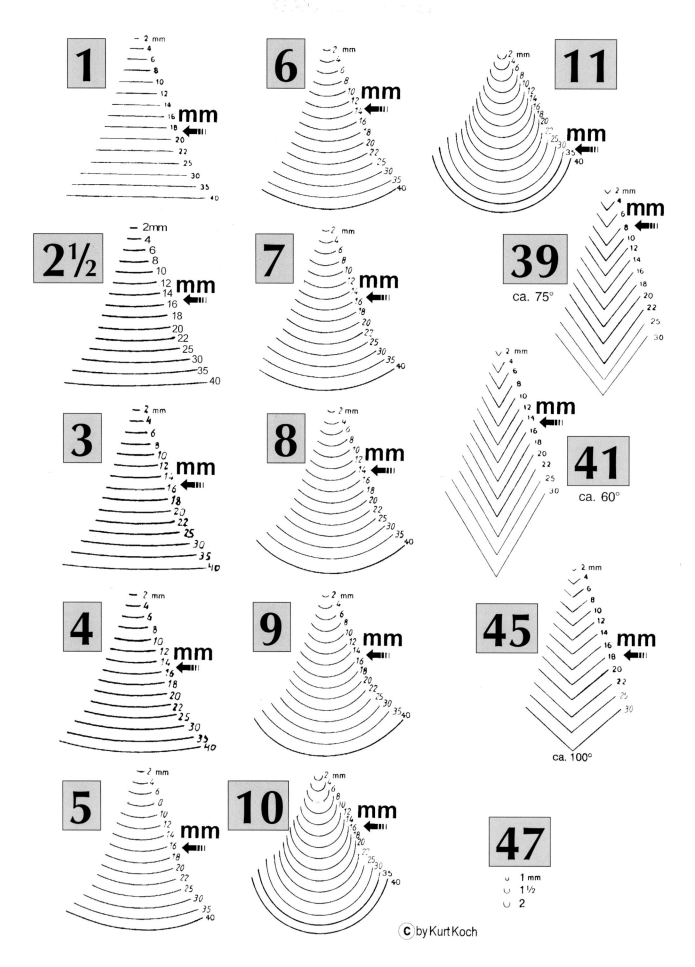

© by Kurt Koch

Project One

This exercise is organized and detailed so that the final ornament appears to be growing out of the background. Therefore, the surrounding wood will be systematically removed to a previously calculated depth. The operation is quite simple, and you always start by cutting out a notch close to, but outside of the selected line of the pattern.

The object of this exercise is to introduce you to wood grain and the effects it will have on your carving. The grain in this example runs horizontally through the pattern. Once you have successfully carved the entire project, I suggest that you repeat the project using a block of wood in which the grain runs vertically through the pattern. You'll learn that you need to plan your cuts to take advantage of the grain.

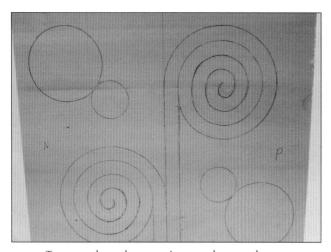

1 Trace or draw the exercises on the wood.

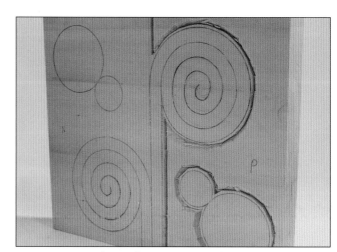

2 Begin with a stab cut just outside the outermost line, about 5 mm deep and at a slight angle away from the ornament. Cut down from the outside toward the deepest point of the stab cut and at an angle of about 45 degrees. The result is a small notch. The shape of the edge of the tools used should more or less correspond to the general shape of the decoration.

The Complete Guide to

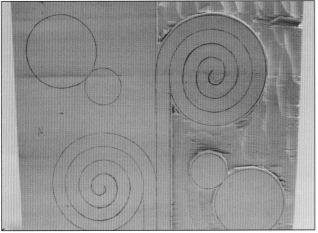

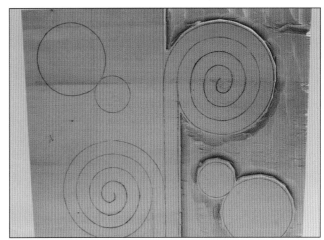

3 In this step, wood will be removed to the depth of the notch using a gouge with a medium deep sweep of not less than 20 mm in width. Repeat this operation here, just as you did in the second step, using a mallet of about 500 grams. The easiest way to rough out the ornament is to cut across the wood grain. To obtain maximum control and depth for each cut, guide your tool so that one side of the edge is always a little bit visible above the wood. If the complete edge is buried in the wood, you will most likely lose control of the cut. Rough out the work to a depth of about 5 mm. Do not yet take the time to clean up the border of the decoration. Finish each notch in its deepest part with short hits—not too strong—with the mallet. Each chip or cutting should fall out by itself. Do not pull, tear or scrape it out. Look where the chip may have some connection, and then cut it free with a well controlled cut. Your growing experience will teach you not to allow excessive wood on the border of the decoration. Otherwise, there will be additional work to do when you finally clean up the border. In no case should you remove all the wood from the border in one single step, nor should you work directly on the pattern line.

4 Continue rough cutting the background by carving a new notch about 5 mm deep. The stab cuts should be directed slightly to the outer side, between 5 to 10 degrees. Do not stab deeply with one single strike. For the beginner, half of the 5 mm depth is just enough. An advantageous rule is to keep the bevel of the tool away from the wood wherever possible. Then, using the same tool, cut toward the stab from a short distance away. Maintain an incline of about 45 degrees. After you finish the small notch, continue to stab until you reach the 5 mm depth. Once again, cut on an incline in the direction of the deepest point of the stab cut until the notch is more or less regular in width and about 5 mm deep.

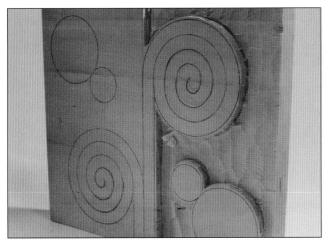

5 Just as in Step 3, cut the wood down to the depth of the notch. The surface plane can and should have a slightly rough structure so that the facets left by the individual cuts are visible. If the individual cuts are obvious in the wood, they are considered "rough structuring." If they are very fine, the surface is considered "polished."

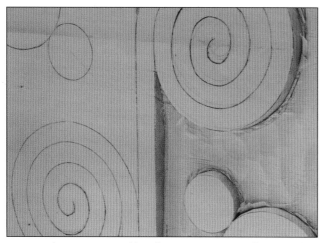

6 The waste wood has been cut away to the intended depth, and the ornament is elevated above the background about 10 mm. Choose a tool with an edge form close to the intended rounding of the finished form of the carved motif for this next step..

Now the borders will be correctly cut in a right angle (90 degrees) to the background. If you don't use a gouge edge that perfectly matches the outer form of your ornament, you will leave a messy and unsightly surface. This is especially true when the radius of the tool profile is smaller than the shape of the ornamental element. If you choose a tool with a profile that is larger than the element, you will have considerably more work to do to obtain a clean, polished surface. Your best choice in this case is to cut finer and finer facets to get a polished surface; although, it is a great deal of extra work and never looks as good.

Make the next perpendicular stab cut 1 mm longer, stabbing into the rough-cut background. This way you will have enough wood to cut a thin layer to clean or even polish the background. At the same time, you will have a clean and precisely cut notch between the perpendicular stab and the horizontal cuts.

It is natural for beginning ornament carvers to have problems with the narrow corners of the ornament. In reality, you cannot cut perfectly clean inside corners with an ordinary flat chisel. The cutting angles of the edges are not suitable for this task, but you can do it with special tools.

Therefore, I suggest small tools with extremely pointed edges. These tools have a very thin blade so that the bevel is very short, permitting you to cut into extremely small and sharp corners. These tools are not suitable and cannot be used to remove thick chips. Always remember that the chips should fall out alone. Normally after cutting, you can blow them out or use a brush. Pay attention to the fact that this exercise is intended to make you practice the stab-and-cut procedures all around the ornament until you are proficient with this basic concept of ornament carving.

7 This photo shows the perfectly cleaned background to this point. Pay close attention to how the individual cuts are placed very regularly next to each other. In this case, it would not look good and is very unprofessional to cross or make irregular cuts. The background should appear as a calming element when the carving is complete, contrary to the living/moving motif of the ornament.

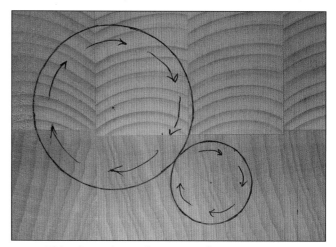

8 This photo shows the cutting directions necessary to carve a hollowed, or concave, circle. Pay attention to the markings in relation to the run of the grain. The cuts will be made across the wood grain. Do not cut parallel with the grain. Observe the cuts from the upper border to the center and from the interior bottom border to the center. Be careful to maintain the same cutting direction on the left and right borders.

The Complete Guide to

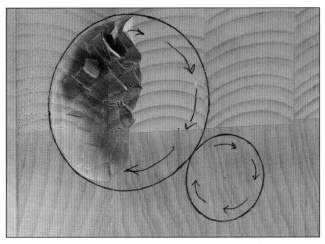

9 The first step in carving a concave circle is to rough out, or waste away, the excess wood. Cut across the grain in the direction of the arrows as you carve the outer edge of the circle.

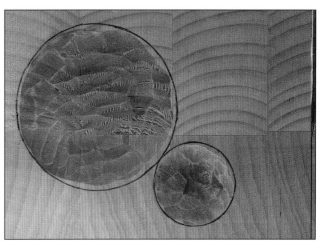

10 Pay close attention to the round border of the ball and to the hollowed center of the ball as you carve.

11 Continue to remove the still visible borders between the individual cuts with finer and finer cuts until you achieve a well polished look.

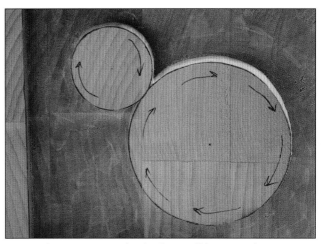

12 These two raised cylinders will be carved into raised segments of a ball. Mark the direction of the cuts on the wood. Cutting in other directions could provoke uncontrolled break outs of the wood.

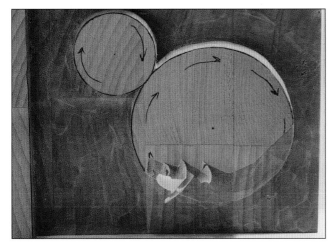

13 Begin carving on the bottom edge of the ball. Take off small portions of wood at a time, remembering to let the chips fall away from the carving naturally.

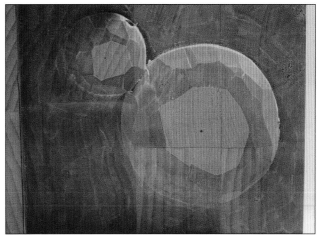

14 This photo shows the rough-cut ball segments. Proceed with ever finer cuts and shavings as you begin to slowly feel the ideal form take shape. Observe the cutting direction(s) at all times that is shown by the arrows. Shortly, the marks are cut away; but, if you are not certain of the direction, mark them in again and again.

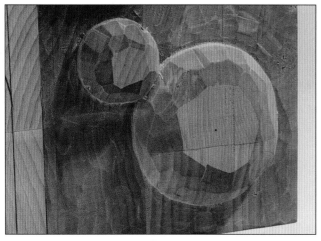

15 Another view of the same step shows the angles of the cuts. Notice that the highest parts of the carving—the centers of the balls—have been left proud.

16 The finished and polished convex shapes are shown in the lower right hand corner. Compare these with the concave circles carved in the upper left hand corner of the block.

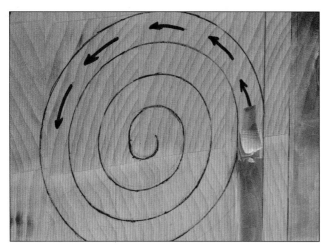

17 Observe that the grain of the wood runs horizontally. This exercise, the recessed helix, or spiral, is cut into "reclined" wood grain. I guarantee that you will have considerable difficulty if you select the wrong cutting directions, so it will help if you pencil in the correct cutting directions on the work piece as shown. Notice that in some places you may have two arrows showing opposite directions. This is not a mistake! It is because you cannot cut to the correct depth in one operation. You must work with at least three different cuts in the marked areas. One is located along the left side, another is along the right side, and one is in the deep center.

18 The carved recessed helix.

19 Three of the four exercises on this practice block are now complete.

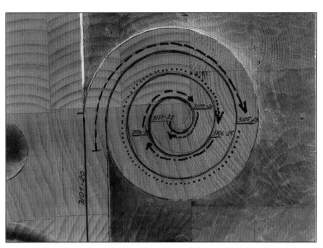

20 Carving the elevated helix will require the following tools, listed from the outside of the spiral in toward the center: Gouge #3105, 25 mm wide; Gouge #3106, 25 mm; Gouge #3106, 30 mm; Gouge #3109, 20 mm and Gouge #3111, 20 mm.

21 First carve the notches according to the pattern lines, carving deeper and wider as you progress to the final polishing of the rounded elements.

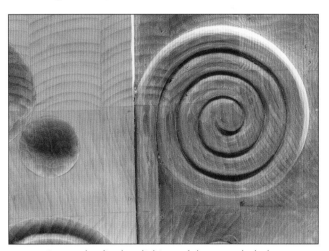

22 Create the final polishing of the rounded elements.

23 A view of the practice block shows all four exercises completed.

24 When photographed at an angle, the light shows the depth and height of the various exercises.

Project Two

Project two is a simple enlarged curve. On each end is something like a knot in the form of a ball segment. One half of the slightly curved knot is cut out in convex form, and the rest of the element is cut out partially in convex form and partially in concave form. The object of this lesson is to teach you a very important rule: When the outer side of a curved element is carved in convex form, the inner side of the curve should be carved concave. This holds true whether the section is wider or narrower than the adjacent element.

Pattern

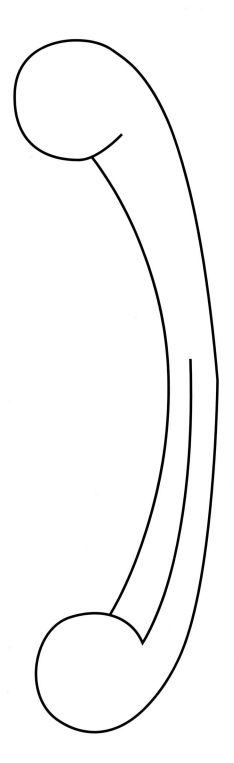

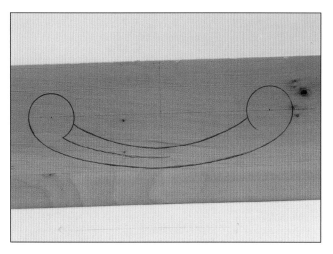

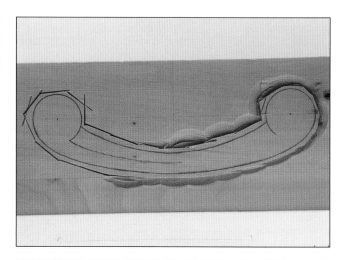

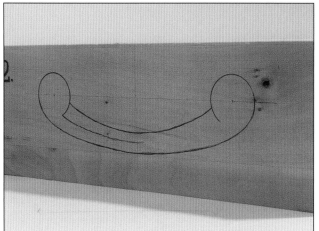

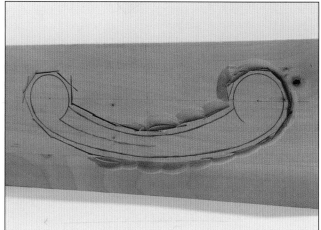

1 Draw or trace the motif on a piece of wood.

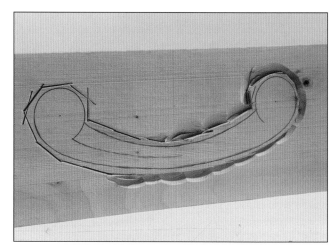

2 About 10 mm of wood needs to be removed from around the ornament to create a new background surface. As in Project One, stab cut vertically to just a short depth. The stab cut line can be a bit rough, as you'll see in the photographs. Cut toward the deepest point of the stab cut at an oblique angle of 45 degrees to create a new notch. The notch is necessary as it eliminates the danger of over-cutting or splitting into the element while you establish a new background.

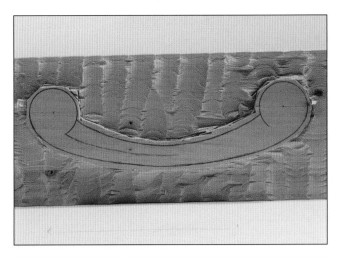

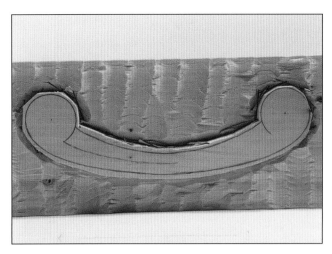

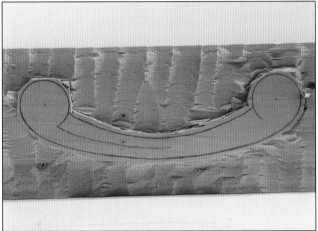

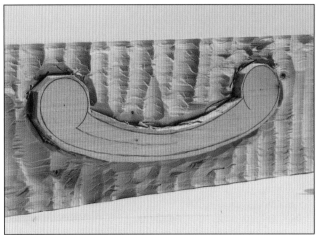

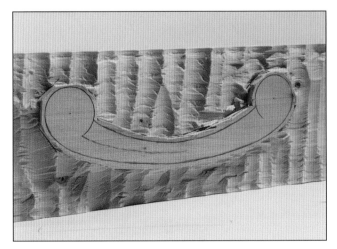

3 Carve a new background plane at the level of the deepest point of the stab cut or notch. The surface structure and the connection with the vertical stab can be a bit rough, but the new plane should appear complementary.

4 Now carve another new notch along the ornament. There are no strong rules for your selection of the carving tools as long as they are appropriate for the task. The cutting edges are just more or less adjusted to the outer shape of the object. You should have now achieved the calculated depth.

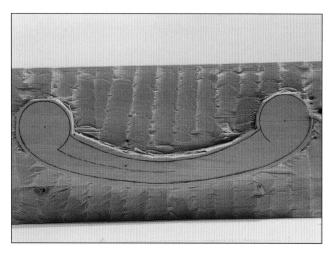

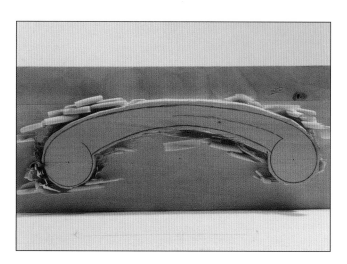

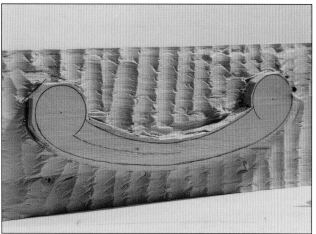

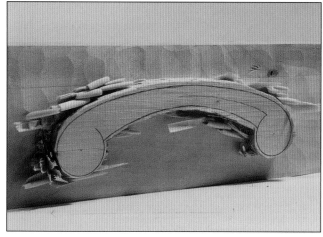

5 Notice that the cuts on the background are run mostly across the wood grain. At the curved border of the ornament, the gouge can be slightly rotated so that the chip will simply drop out.

6 The result to this point is a slightly curved edge against a perfectly plain new background. The final structure is weakly expressed and the cut borders are almost invisible.

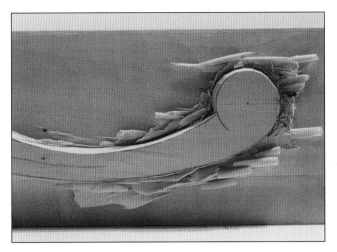

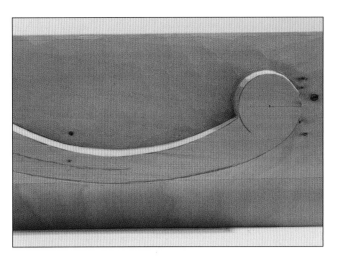

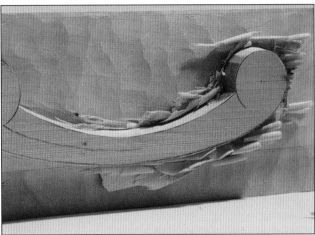

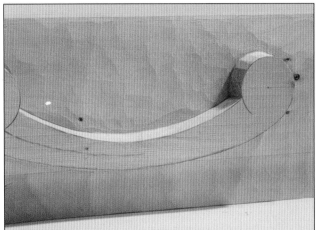

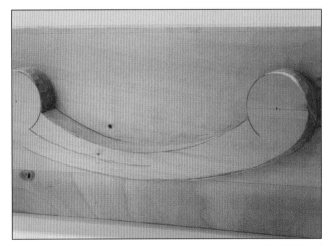

7 Now the outline of the element is stab cut rather exactly and perfectly vertical, at a right angle to the background. Match the gouge's cutting edge as closely as possible the outer shape of the ornament.

8 The sides of the ornament are now completely free from the background. It is important to do this in the same way in all similar future exercises. The more precise you are in the preparation work, the better and more exact the ornament's shape will be. Exactness here will also simplify the modeling work to come. Don't ever think that more or less depth will be correct. This is a common error in logic that occurs to most people.

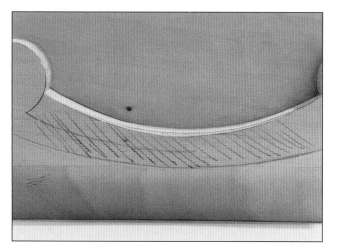

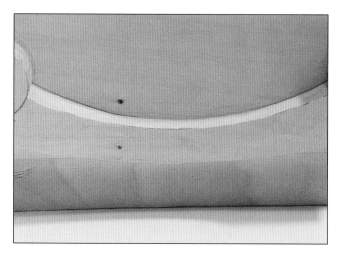

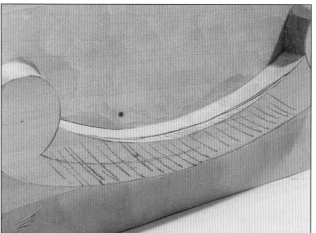

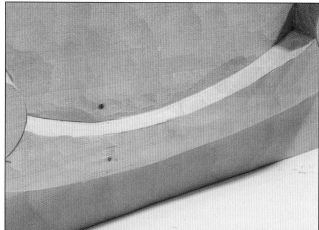

9 At this point, I suggest that you begin marking in pencil the cuts that will need to be made prior to making them. To cut or to stab should be marked clearly at each step of the carving process. As you'll see from the various views, these pencil marks should be drawn not only on the top of the ornament, but also down the sides as well. The first step is to remove wood as marked from the narrow portion of the ornament.

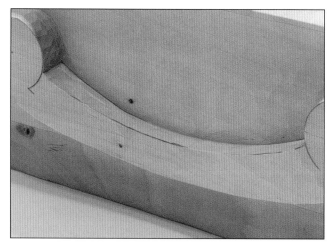

10 In general, the photos of the completed work were taken at the same angles as the photos showing the marked-up ornament. This way you can better follow and compare the results from the individual steps. Notice how the pencil marks have been carved away to thin the middle of the ornament.

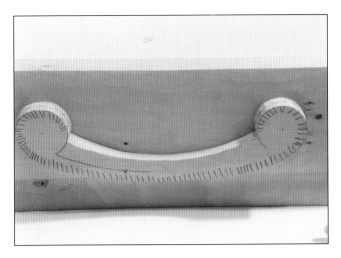

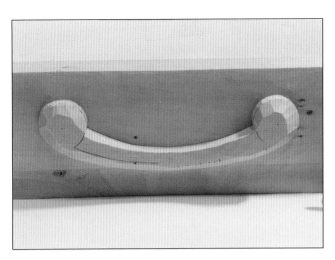

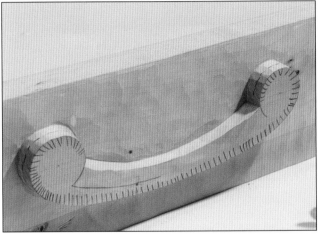

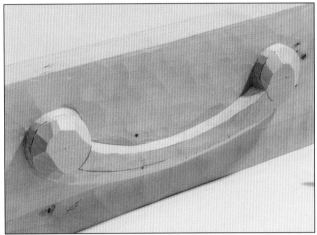

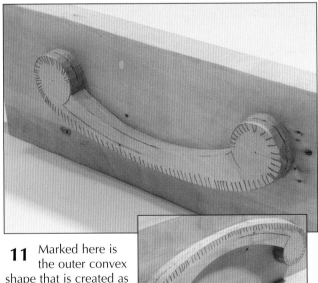

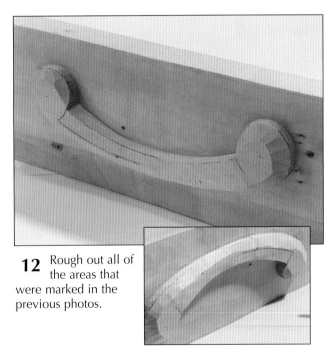

11 Marked here is the outer convex shape that is created as described in the introduction to this project and done according to the rules of ornament carving. Note the dashed pencil line partway down the ornament. This marks the depth at which the convex shape begins.

12 Rough out all of the areas that were marked in the previous photos.

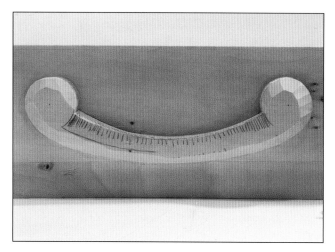

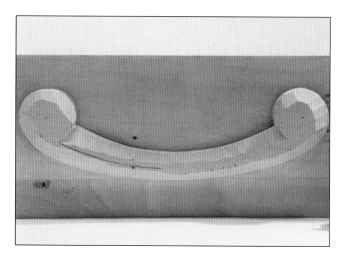

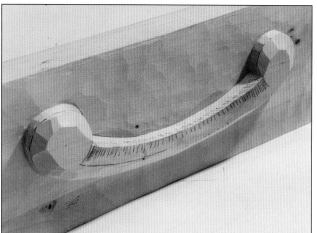

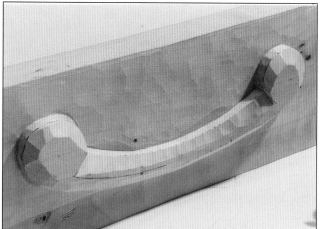

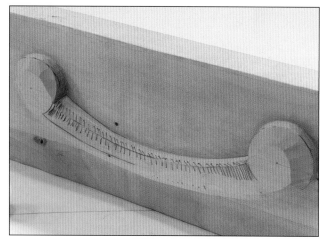

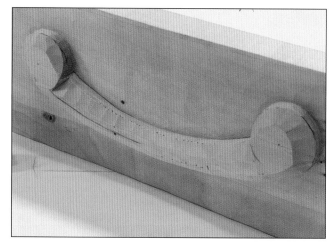

13 Pencil in the next cuts. This step will remove wood from the inside curve of the ornament.

14 The ornament should now look like this.

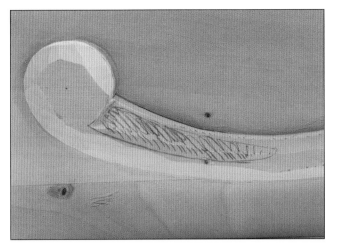

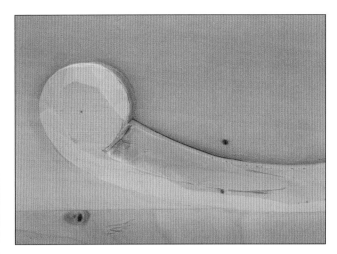

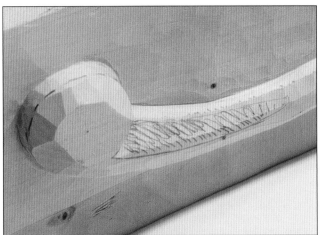

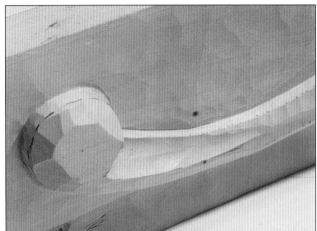

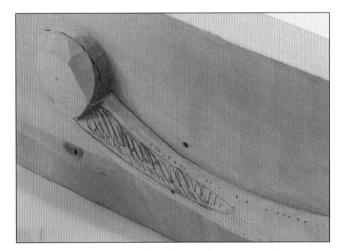

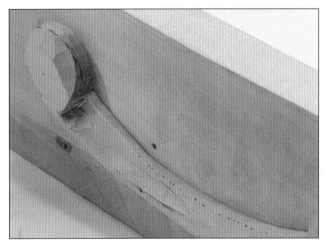

15 By our previous rule, the inside curve will be carved concave. In order to give you more chances to practice, I have formed the right section as a rounded element. There is great value to this practice because there are cuts against and with the wood grain. Mark the left section to be carved with a concave form.

16 The result of the concave cuts is shown here. These cutting exercises should be done with utmost concentration and must be absolutely perfect. Perfection comes only with careful practice. With practice you will be able to feel—almost automatically—when the cut does not run correctly. This "feel" will help you to recognize immediately when the cut does not follow your intentions. If a cut is going awry, immediately stop and cut from the opposite side. If there is no possibility to do this, perhaps because there is no space, then try the cut from the side.

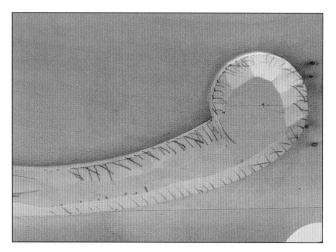

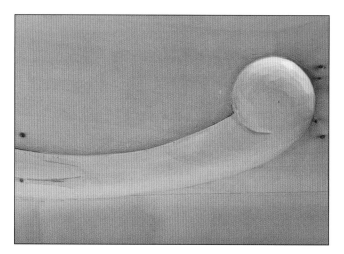

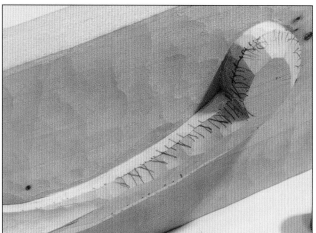

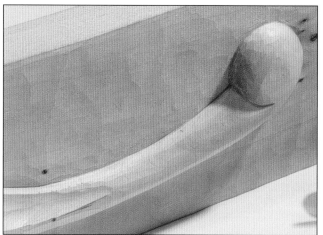

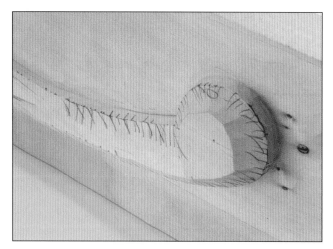

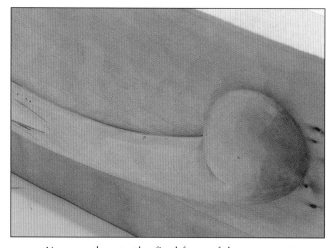

17 Mark the wood to be removed from the right side of the ornament. These cuts will round the edges of the convex areas.

18 You are close to the final form of the ornament. The right side should now be polished with very fine cuts.

Many kinds of wood have a lively animated grain structure with many visible colors. If you are using a wood like this—oak, ash and chestnut are good examples—it is easier to recognize the direction of the grain. With basswood, alder, birch and similar woods in which the grain is not as visible, you must learn to sense the grain intuitively. Learn the feel of the grain as you cut, as this will help you to understand the mechanics of the wood.

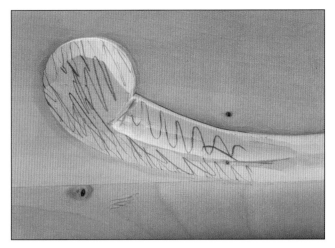

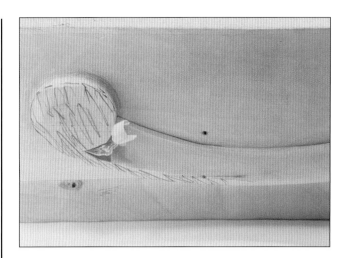

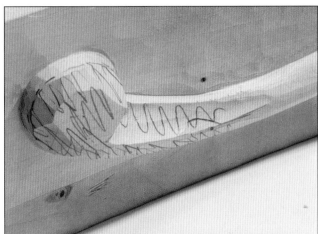

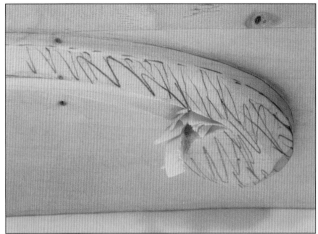

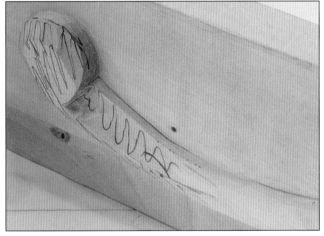

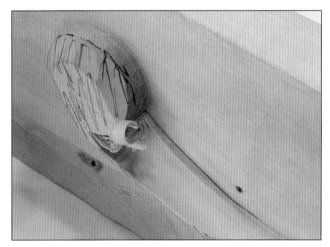

19 Finish the exercise by marking the wood to remove from the left (concave) side of the element.

20 As always, but especially here, make a great effort to achieve precision cuts and clean corners.

I will repeat these words over and over as we proceed, because I feel they impart an important lesson in woodcarving. The effect and the artistic value of a carved ornament, or of any woodcarving for that matter, is dependent on the precision and clean lines of the finished work. The contrary would not in any way be considered a professional piece, just sloppy work.

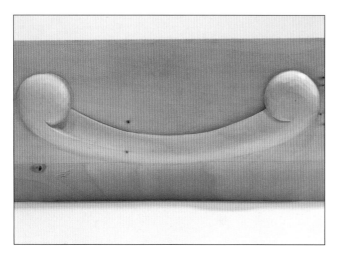

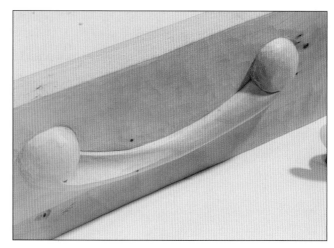

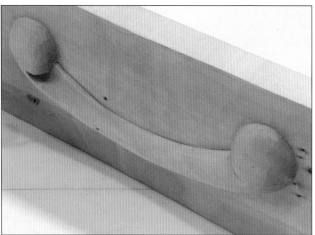

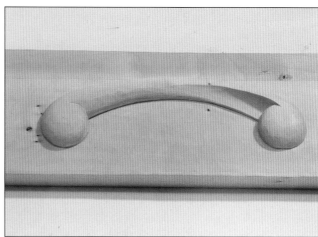

21 Project Two is complete. The photos here show the ornament from different views and under different lighting conditions so that you can get an overall picture of the finished piece. Once again: The accuracy of the cuts brings cleanness and precision to the ornament and is an essential part of the quality. Don't allow any rough part at any place and particularly not in the borders of the cuts. Any residual chips or areas where the ornament is not well polished detract from the finished work. Clean up the last small remnants of the carving using small, fine chip knives with sharp and pointed edges.

Project Three

This project is an adaptation of the previous exercise. The convex ball segment appears only on the left side of the ornament. The right side of the ornament includes three elements, two of which are concave and convex, and one of which is only convex. The object of this exercise is to bring together the concave and convex elements that were introduced in the previous exercise.

Pattern

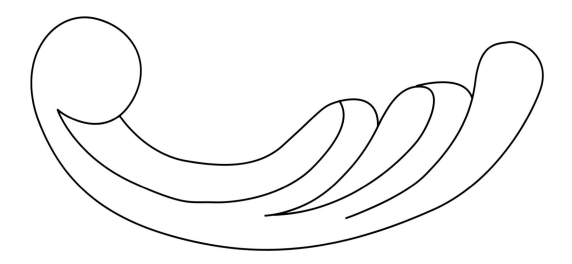

1 Trace the design on the wood. Here you can see the simple elements just as they are to be carved.

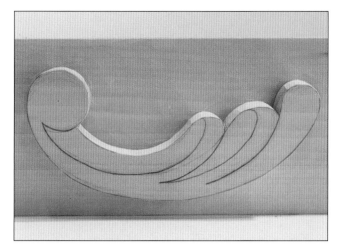

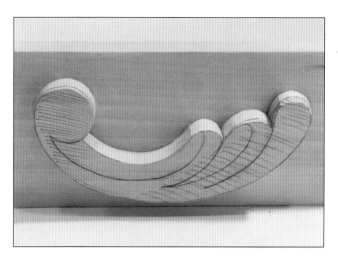

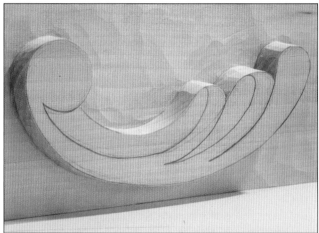

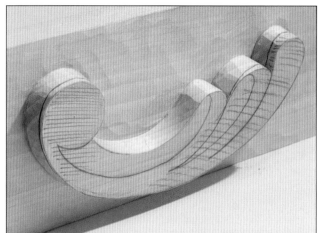

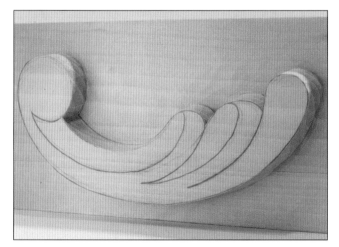

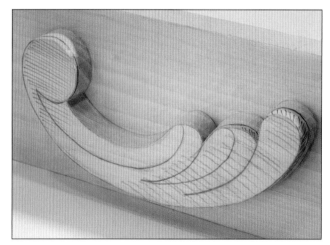

2 Because the initial steps of relieving the ornament from the background are the same throughout the rest of the exercises, I will no longer include specific instructions for these steps. The process of outlining the ornament with a gouge, making the notch, and removing the background up to the ornament are part of the basics learned and practiced in the first two projects. Notice that this step shows the motif with stab cuts completed and then cut cleanly. It is identical in shape to the pattern that was drawn on the wood in Step 1.

3 Mark the wood to be removed. Remember that these pencil marks should indicate the shape and the depth of the cuts to take place.

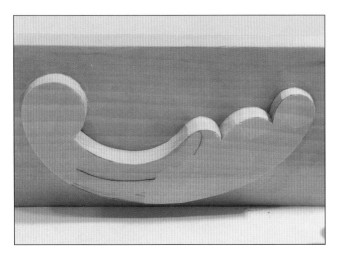

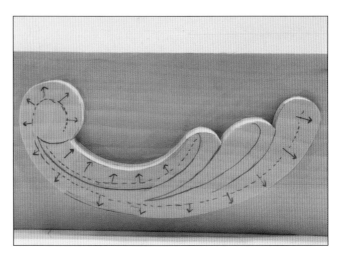

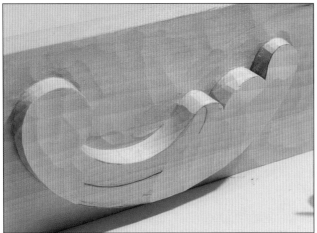

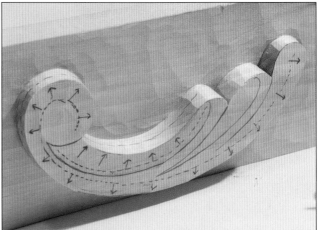

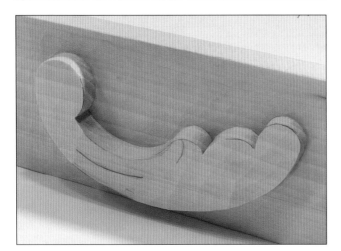

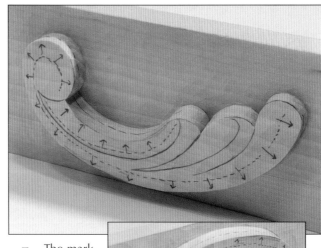

4 These photos show the results after the wood has been removed. Notice that the element on the far right of the photo has been lowered the most.

5 The markings on this step show the orientation of the cuts according to the final shape that we want. The knot, the convex curve on the outer edge and the concave curve on the inner edge are all marked. The arrows mark the actual directions of the cuts. Again, notice the dashed line around the vertical plane of the ornament that shows how deep the cuts should go.

The Complete Guide to

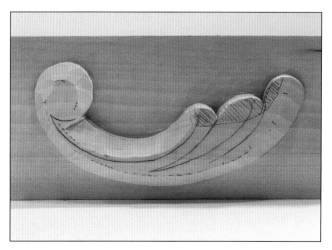

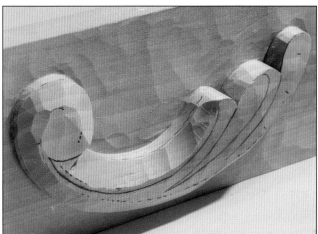

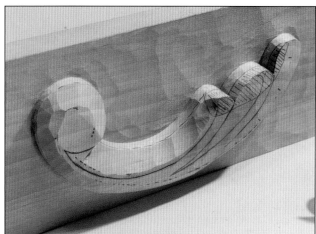

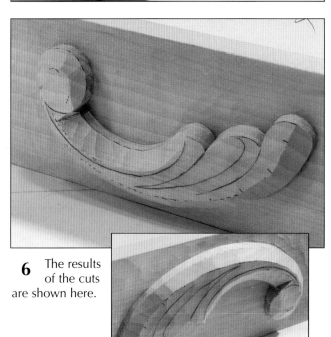

6 The results of the cuts are shown here.

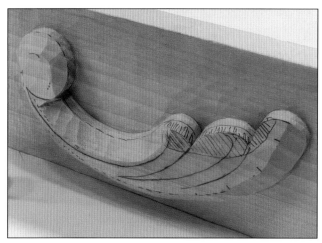

7 Mark the wood to be removed from the tips of the three elements on the right side of the ornament. Study the final project photo at the beginning of this section before carving the next steps. Notice the finished ends of the two elements on the inner curve. They are formed as spoons. The third element on the outer edge of the curve is convex and shaped like a tongue.

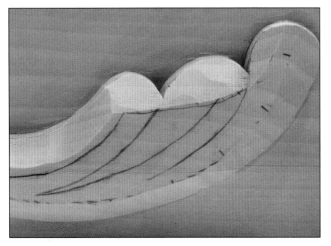

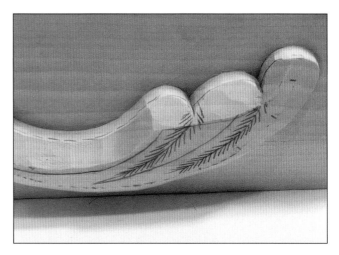

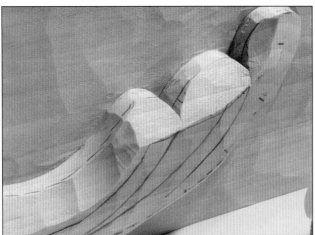

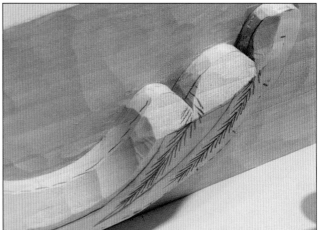

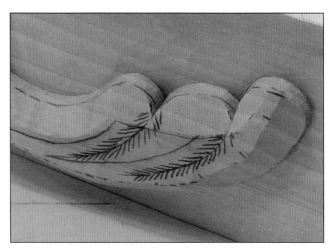

8 The results of the first portion of wood to be removed from the three elements are shown here.

9 This step shows you how to carve an optical separation of the curved elements. Study the final photo of the project at the beginning of this section, then mark the wood to be removed as indicated.

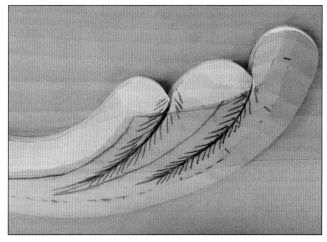

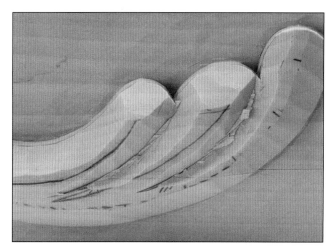

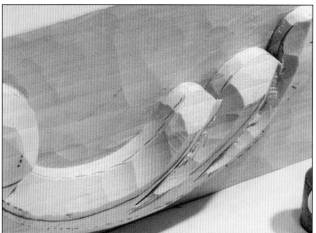

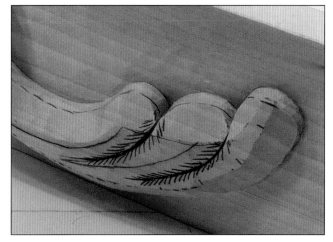

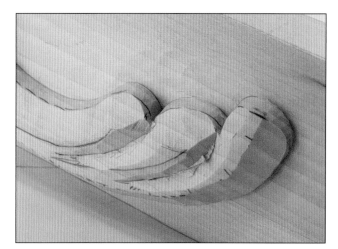

10 The first step is to create a center vertical cut between the elements as shown in this photograph.

11 Next carve a roughly cut notch. Always use the largest possible sizes of tools/edges for this and similar work.

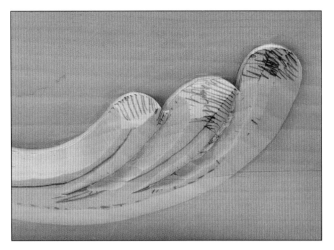

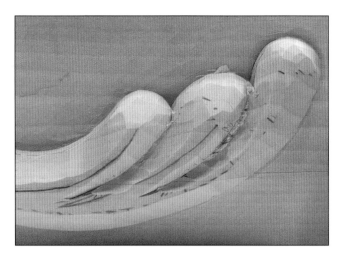

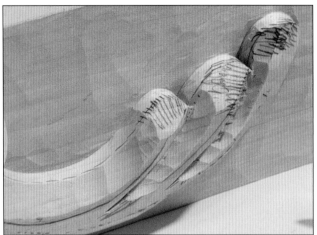

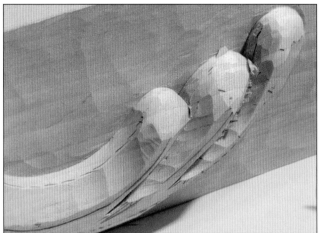

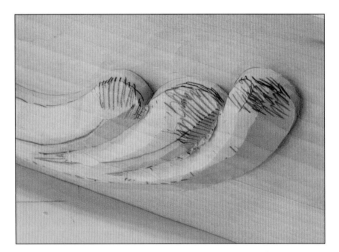

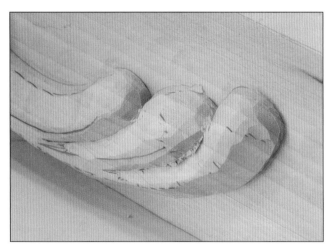

12 Mark the ends of the individually curved elements for wood removal as shown. The ends of these three elements will be ball-shaped.

13 The results of the cuts are shown here. Again, try to cut correctly. Be careful to remove the correct amount of wood and to use the correct amount of pressure on the tool. Not taking care in this area could mean costly mistakes.

The Complete Guide to

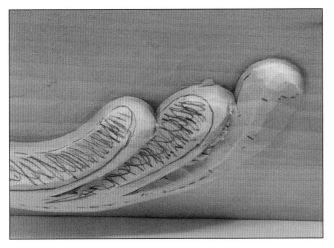

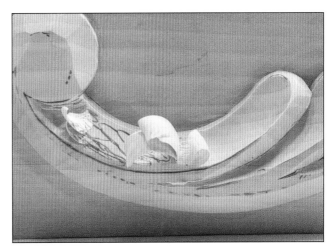

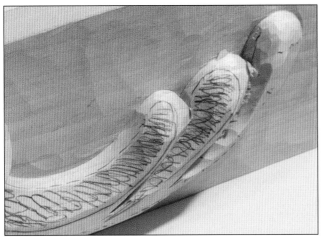

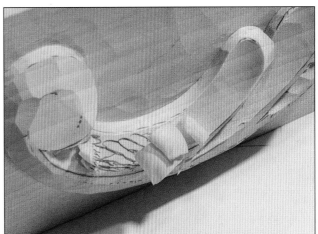

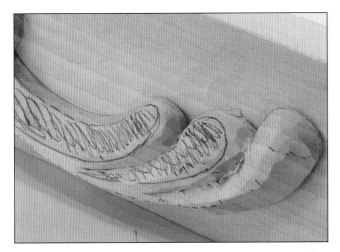

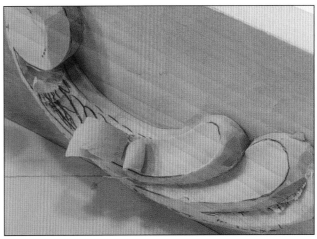

14 According to the rules given in Project Two regarding the location of convex and concave shapes on curves, mark the wood to be carved away on the inner sides of the two innermost elements. (Rule: The inner side of the curves are always carved to the concave form and the outer curves to the convex form.)

15 Make the concave cuts at the ends of the elements first. Pay close attention to the changes in cutting direction near the knot. Begin carving near the knot and create some space by diagonally cutting a starting point for the longer concave cuts.

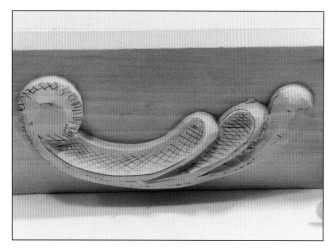

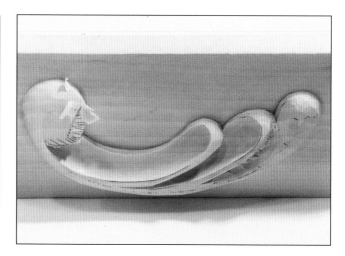

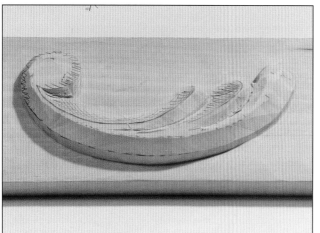

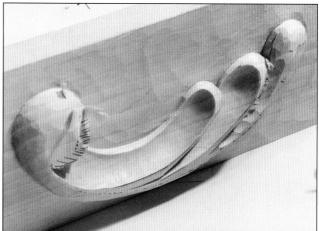

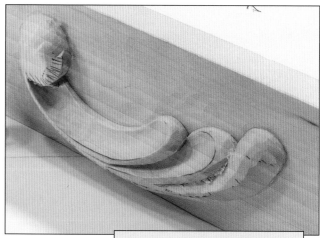

16 The next step is to further define the knot and the concave cuts. The cutting edge of your gouge must match the depth of the cut—not too wide and not too flat. In these curved elements, the concave cuts have parallel borders and the depth is without variation.

17 The results of the cuts are shown in these photographs. It is to your best advantage to first carve the concave parts, and then carve the convex outer

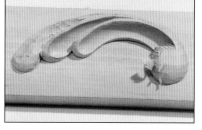

curves. In this way you have a chance to adapt and to combine the best carving lines, something you would not be able to do if you work out the convex forms first.

The Complete Guide to

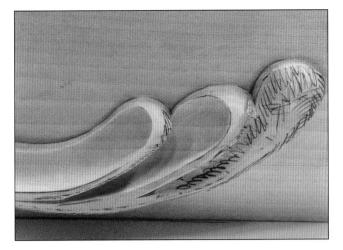

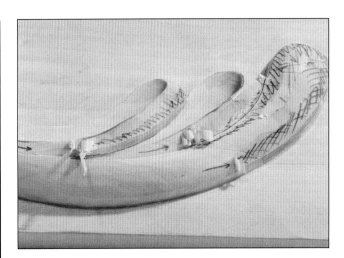

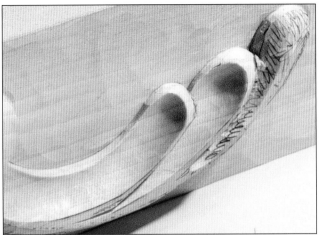

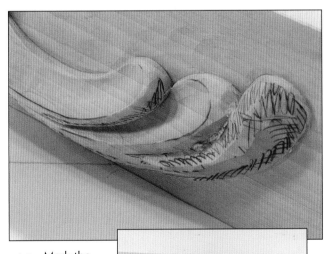

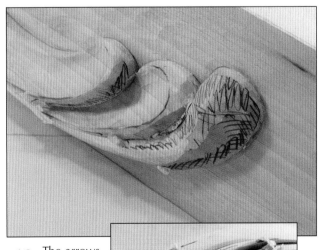

18 Mark the wood to be removed from the outermost convex element and from the sides of the inner two elements as shown.

19 The arrows show the direction of the cuts in these areas. Remove small, thin sections of wood as you carefully shape these areas.

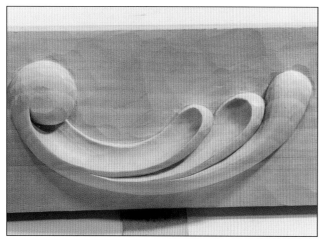

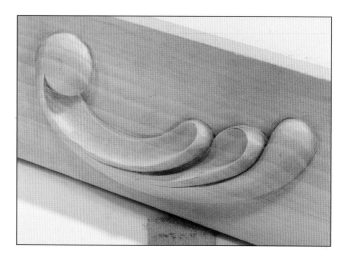

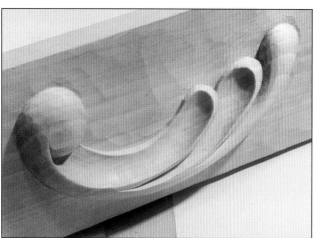

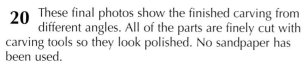

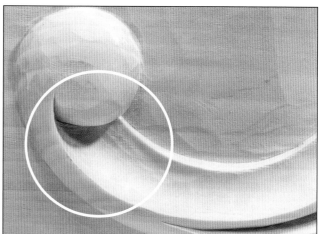

20 These final photos show the finished carving from different angles. All of the parts are finely cut with carving tools so they look polished. No sandpaper has been used.

At this point, let's take a minute to talk about specialty tools. As you progress, you will quickly find out that it is much easier to use specialty tools. For example, it is much more difficult to cut a perfect connection in the concave form of the knot using a gouge shaped with a "tongue." (See the area circled in white.) These connections, called "unification of elements," are mostly found in the decorative elements of ornamental woodcarving. On a regular gouge, the deepest point of the gouge, the center, is pushed forward, and the wings of the gouge are tapered back. This formation gives the cutting edge something of a rounded form when viewed from above. The result is a slightly formed "tongue" that is more prominent on deeper gouges and less prominent on shallow gouges.

To work with ornaments the opposite is true. The wings (or corners of the cutting edge) extend forward and the center of the gouge recedes in a sort of concave shape. This is the same shape, although this is a little bit more difficult, that you need to maintain with a v-tool.

The unification of elements that I mentioned above is the reason for using these concave cutting-edge tools when doing ornamental carving.

It is far easier and quicker to work with a properly shaped tool. Conversely, it is better to carve the concave curves (See the area in the white rectangle.) if you use tools ground with the tongue slightly forward.

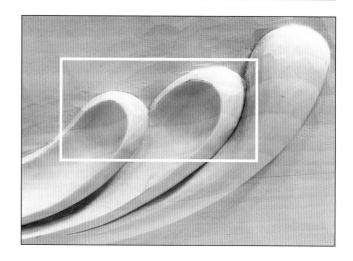

Project Four

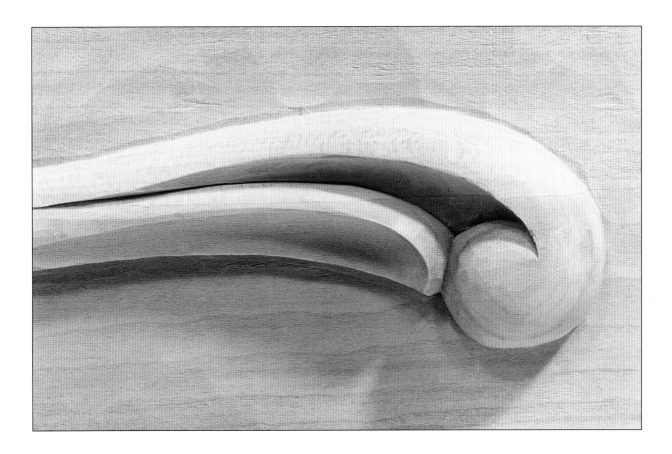

The object of this exercise is to show you how one element can be split into individual elements.

The surrounding parts near the knot are similar to a tongue adjacent to the knot, like the tongue and knot you carved in Project Three. These areas are carved according to the rules governing curves. (Rule: The inner side of the curves are always carved to the concave form and the outer curves to the convex form.).

The reality is that where there is an outer curve, there is always an inner curve. Many curves can be integrated together or joined side by side. Notice in this example: On the inside of the outer curve is located an inner curve, and this is consequently a concave element.

Pattern

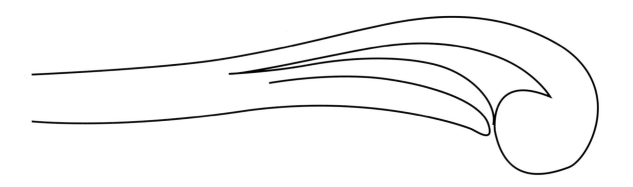

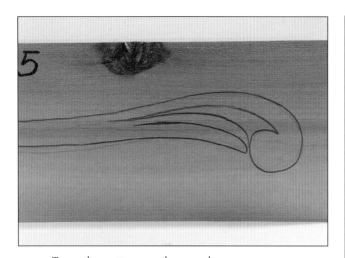

1 Trace the pattern on the wood.

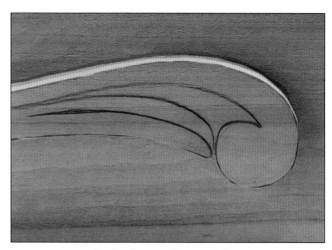

2 Remove the background around the ornament.

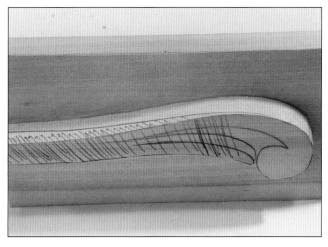

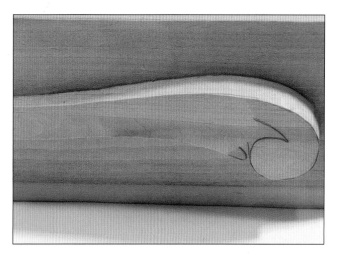

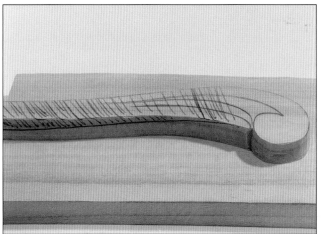

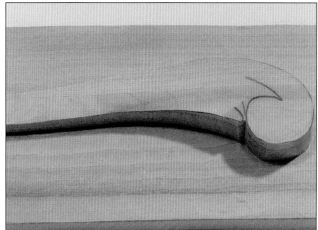

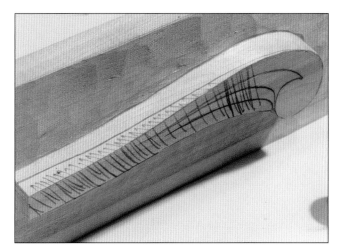

3 Mark the wood to be removed.

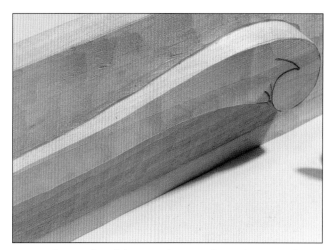

4 The results of the wood removal are shown in these photographs.

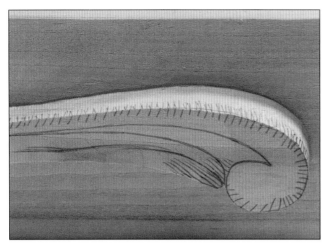

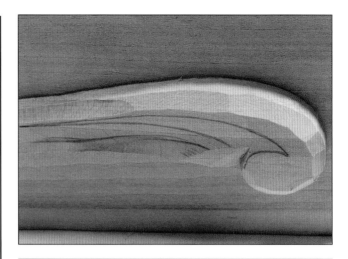

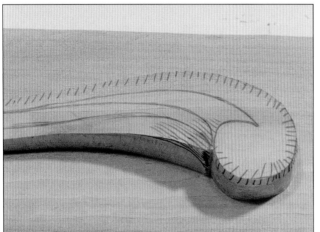

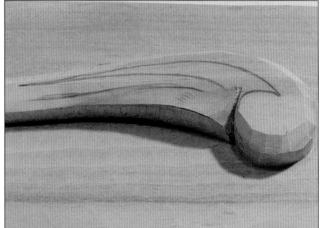

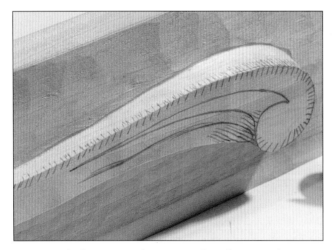

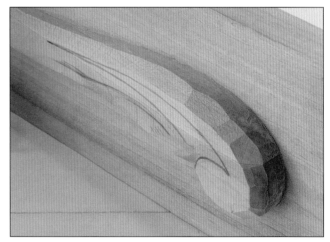

5 Mark the areas to be removed as shown in these photographs.

6 The results of the cuts are shown here.

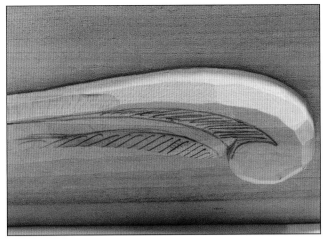

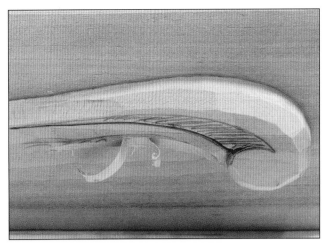

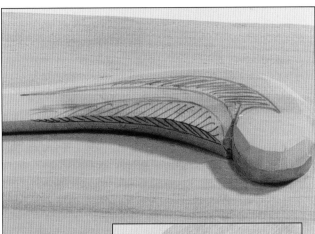

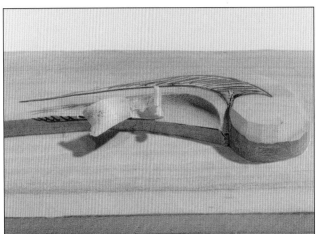

7 Before continuing, study the finished project at the beginning of this section. A curve always requires two carving techniques. The rules are fixed: Outside curves are convex and inside curves are concave. If more than one curve exists as an element, or if curves of elements are side by side, then the rule is still valid when changing from concave (inner side) to convex (outer side) curves. A wider curve element can be split into individual elements (such as in this project) to maintain the liveliness and the feeling of movement. By rule, each new inner side will be carved out in a concave form.

When changing from one curve to the opposite curve (perhaps from a right curve to a left curve), the carving technique is changed also. The concave form is changing almost invisibly and very elegantly into the convex carved form. It occurs the same way on the opposite side of the element when the convex carving changes to concave. Both locations where concave carving is necessary are marked.

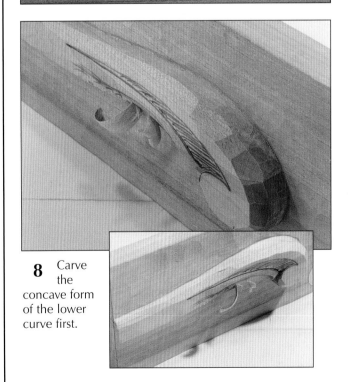

8 Carve the concave form of the lower curve first.

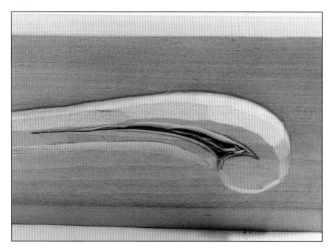

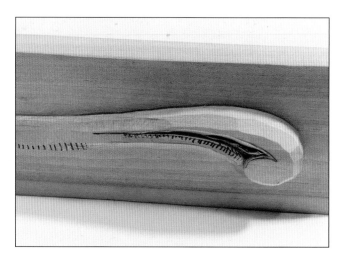

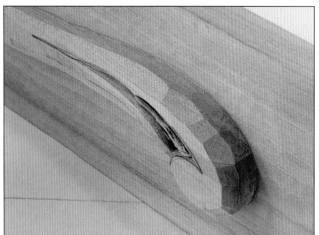

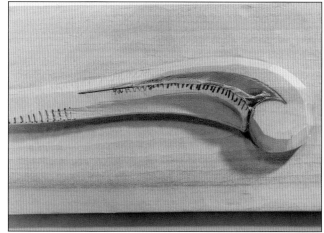

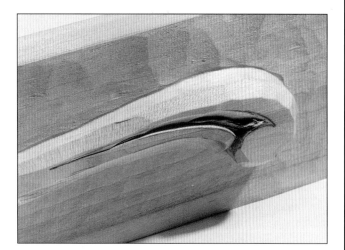

9 Carve the concave form of the upper curve next. Notice that this is a much narrower concave form than the concave form in the previous photo.

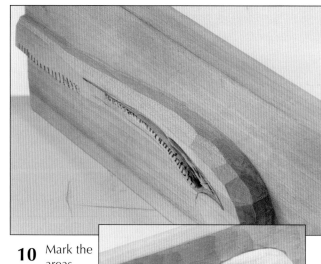

10 Mark the areas from which wood will be removed as shown in the photographs. These areas will be convex.

The Complete Guide to

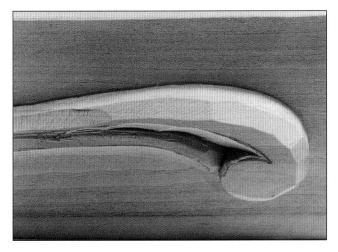

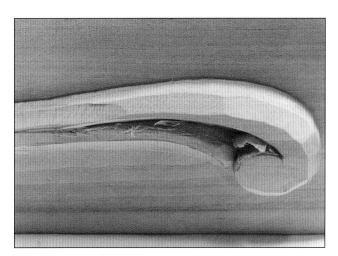

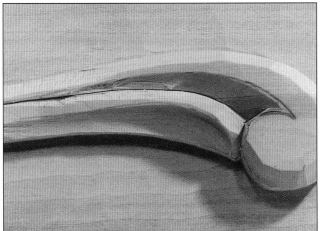

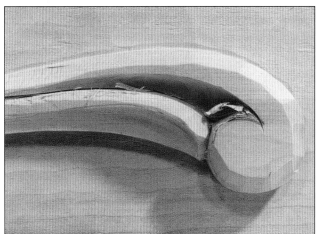

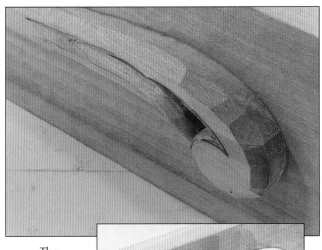

11 The results of the cuts are shown in these photographs.

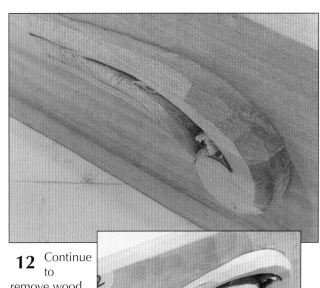

12 Continue to remove wood from the concave areas, carefully shaping the form.

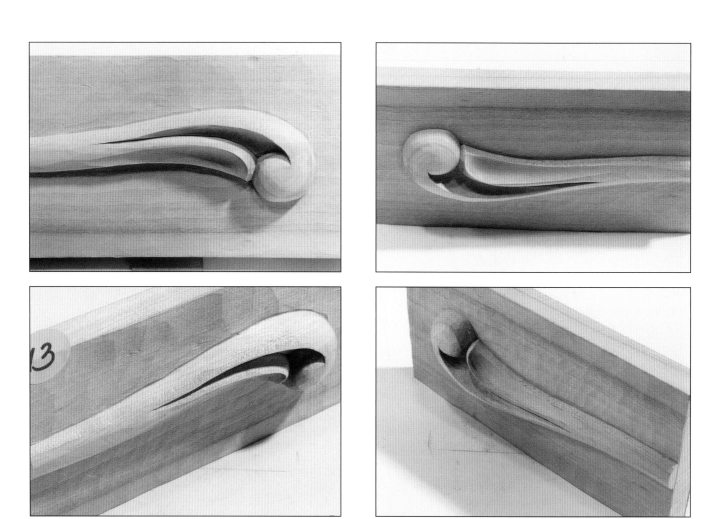

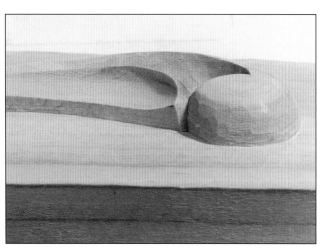

13 The final ornament is shown from several angles, including upside down. Again, strive to achieve unconditional quality and cleanliness. Do not enter into compromises. The correct tool is always very important, but even with the best quality and the best assortment of tools, it always depends on what you do with the tools. To the beginner, it may seem that I excessively stress these repeated warnings and advice. But once you are an accomplished ornament carver, then you will remember my warnings with pleasure. The closer you follow my instructions in this basic phase, the quicker you will come to be a competent expert. But if you are careless now, your way in the future will be much more difficult. So I urge you: Pay strict attention to develop an always elegant flow of lines, inner edges and outer edges.

Project Five

Project Five has a multiple structure and represents an independent decoration. With each new step of the carving, think about the never resting lines and forms. The lines are or should be always in movement.

Pattern

1 Trace the pattern on the wood.

The Complete Guide to

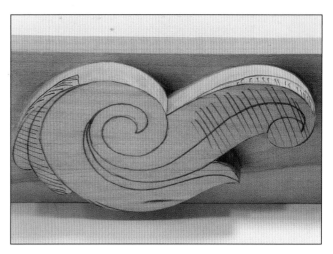

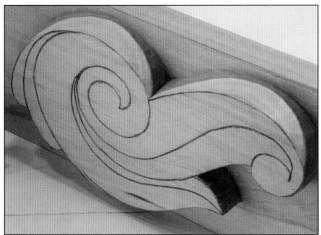

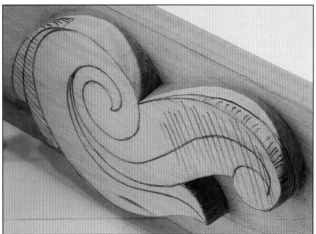

2 The rough carving necessary to free the motif from the background is not demonstrated. Be sure to be exact in your cuts as you work to free the motif.

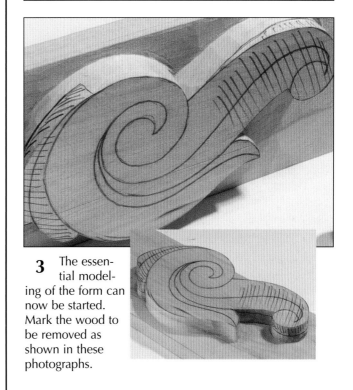

3 The essential modeling of the form can now be started. Mark the wood to be removed as shown in these photographs.

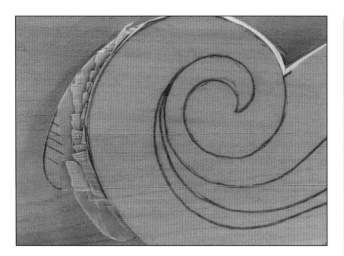

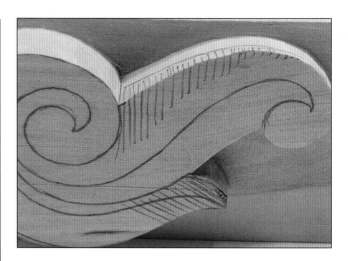

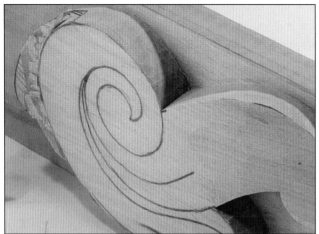

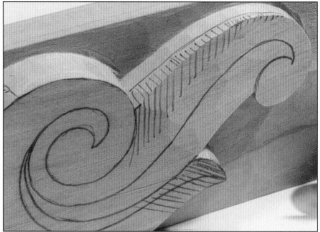

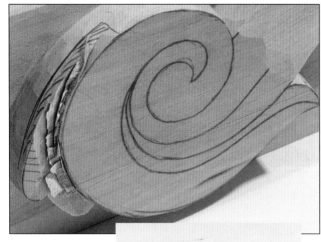

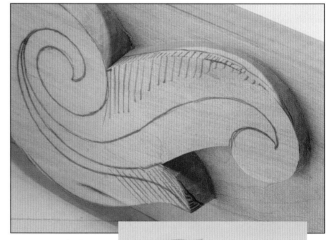

4 The results of the cuts can be seen here. The views from different angles should help with your interpretation.

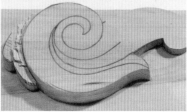

5 Mark the next areas for wood removal. Pay special attention to this motif. Study the final photo at the beginning of the section to see how the convex cuts interchange with the concave cuts. Each outer curve starts with the convex form and glides elegantly into the concave form once the curve is inverted.

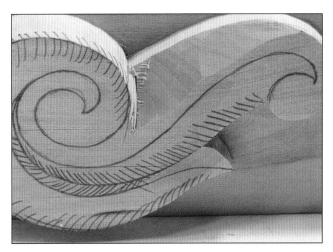

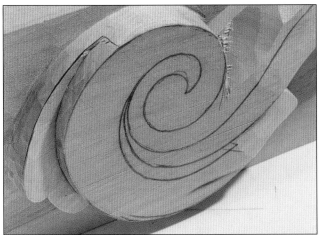

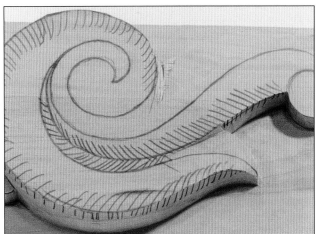

7 The notches between the curved elements should be done next.

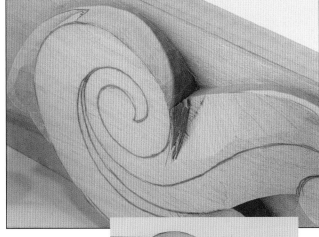

6 These photos show the results of the cuts. The general depth is more or less 15 mm to 18 mm.

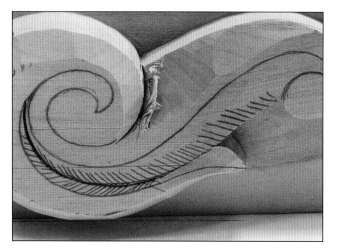

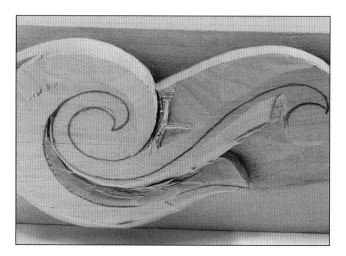

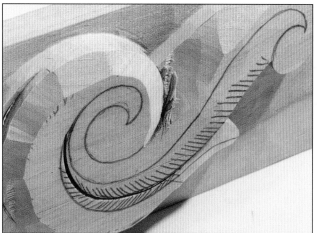

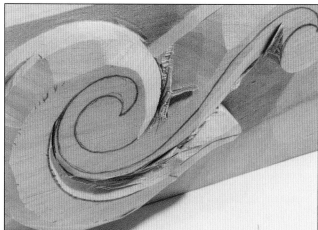

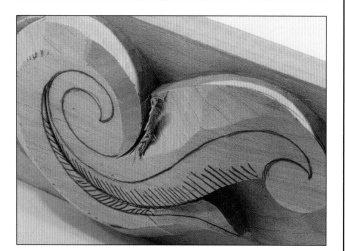

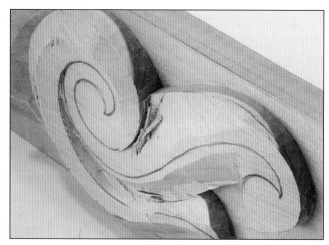

8 Directly on the pattern lines between the curves, stab vertically. Make the stab cut deeper on the places where the carving is deeper, but don't stab as deep where the curve is much more narrow. This way you will have better control when you cut the borders clean, as the wood must not be broken out. Again, don't use force to free chips if they are not already cut free. Cut them out, don't tear them out.

9 Continue removing wood from the notches between the curves.

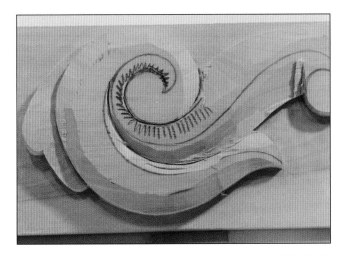

11 Here you can see the wood removed. Because of the many curves and turns involved in this motif, you can practice the correct cutting direction with respect to the grain and shape of the ornament, i.e., with the grain, across the grain, into the grain, and so on. Around the central knot, you will need to change tools more and more frequently to match the profile of the curve.

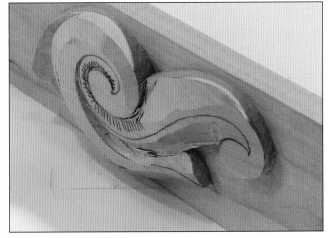

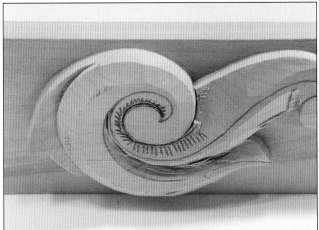

10 Mark the very center of the motif for wood removal.

 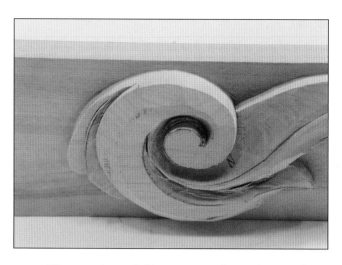

12 The rough carving from the previous step is continued.

13 The top photo of this sequence shows the wood to be removed in this step. The bottom two photos show the wood removed.

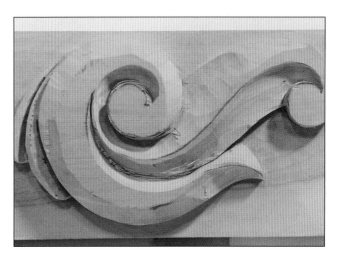

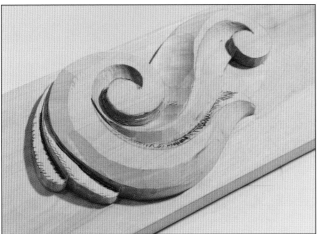

14 Again, the top photo shows the wood to be removed; the bottom photo shows the motif after the wood has been removed. These smaller cuts are the last preparatory cuts before the modeling of the final form. Notice how the decorative edges on the left side of the motif have been marked for rounding.

15 The top photo shows the final preparatory cuts. The photo below shows the motif after the cuts have been made. Notice that the decorative edges on the left side of the motif have been slightly rounded. These areas are convex on the finished project.

16 The finished ornament is shown from a number of views, including an upside-down view. Study these various shots to help you as you remove thinner and thinner slivers of wood to "polish" the final motif.

Project Six

With this ornament, we move to applying the concave and convex surfaces to natural objects such as flowers. This partially stylized flower includes a realistic-looking flower on top with free-flowing elements below that are reminiscent of the previous five projects. The combination of these parts results in a well-designed ornamental carving of a floral element. There is not enough movement or life in the border of the flower alone. Only because of the variety and life of the fully formed center of the flower is the boredom of the border somewhat compensated. The lively movement of the decorations below ensures the appeal of the design.

As you carve, remember the following: Movement is the beginning and the end of all ornamental carving. When you do not create this feeling of movement, the most properly carved work is literally destroyed.

Pattern

1 Trace or draw the pattern on the wood.

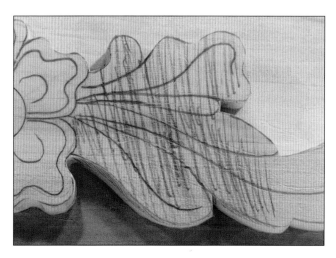

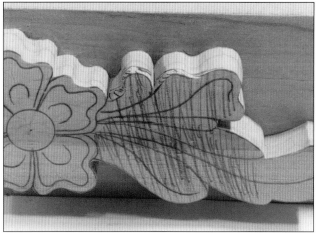

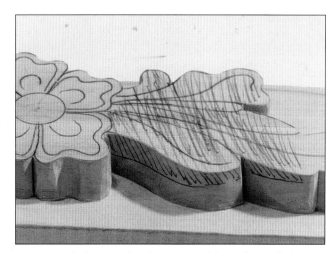

2 Remove the wood surrounding the ornament by outlining, creating notches, and carving away wood until the background is smooth and the ornament stands free.

3 Mark the wood to be removed from the surface of the lower elements. Study the finished carving at the beginning of this section prior to carving the different elements and levels. Your studies will be advantageous in forming movement and life within the total image and presentation. Liveliness and movement provide the mystic beauty of this style of woodcarving.

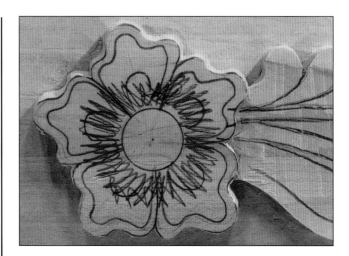

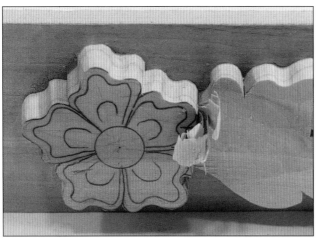

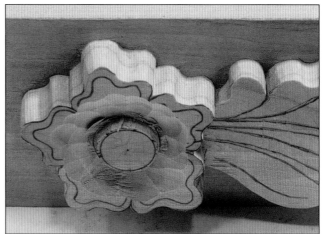

4 The results of the cuts are shown in these photos. Notice how the cuts are angled deeper toward the head of the flower. Remember, chips should be allowed to fall freely from the carving. They should not be pulled or torn free.

5 The top photo shows the center of the flower's petals marked for wood removal. The curves of the ornament's lower elements have been redrawn according to the original pattern. The lower two photos show the results of the cuts.

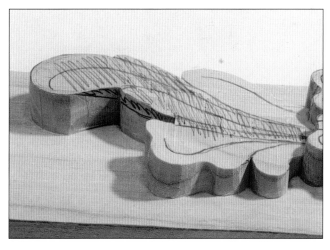

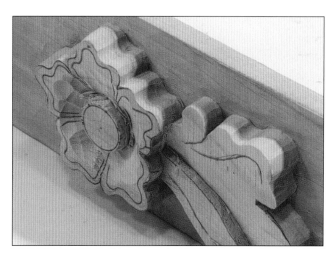

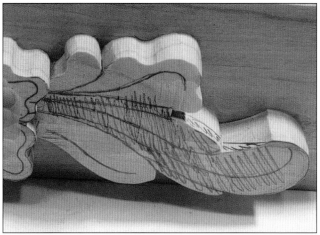

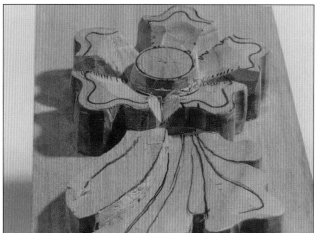

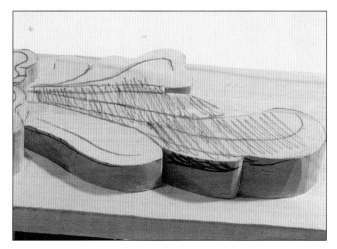

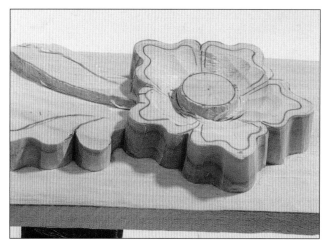

6 Mark the wood to be removed in the next step as shown in these photographs. As in previous projects, note that the markings are not only on the surface of the ornament but also on the sides as well.

7 The results of the cuts are seen in these photos. The main function of this step is to separate the lower elements, one from the other.

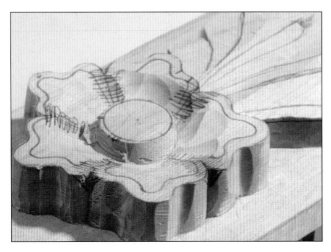

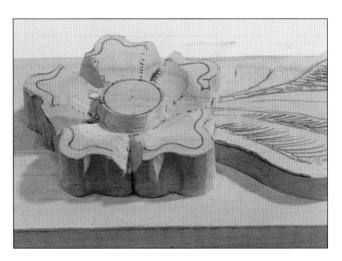

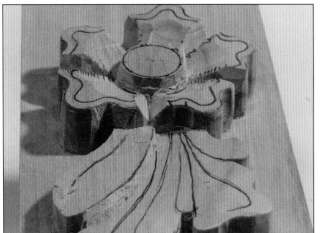

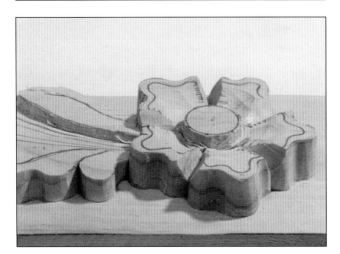

8 The top photo shows the wood to be removed from between the flower's petals. Note also that the individual elements on the lower portion of the ornament have been redrawn. The bottom two photos show the results of these cuts.

9 The top photo shows the wood to be removed from the lower elements. The bottom two photos show the results of the cuts. Notice that all of these cuts are concave cuts marking the inside areas of the curves.

The Complete Guide to

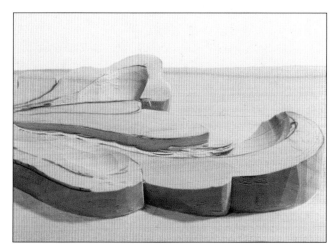

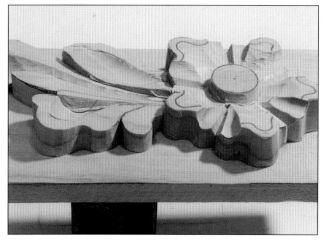

10 These photos show the wood to be removed in the next step. Note that wood will be removed from both sides of each petal. These cuts form the concave areas that border the interior section of each petal. Again, the marks are made on the surface of the ornament as well as on the sides.

11 This series of photos shows the results of the cuts.

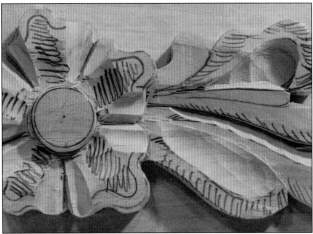

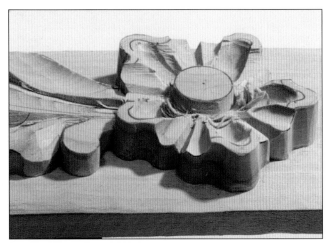

12 Mark the wood to be removed in the next step. These areas encompass the outer edges of the lower elements and the concave areas that form the interiors of the petals.

13 These photos show the results of the cuts.

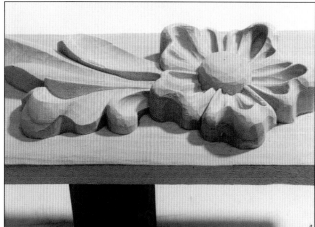

14 The last rough cuts to be made should be marked as shown in the top photo. The results of these cuts are shown in the bottom two photos.

15 Continue to polish the shape with finer and finer cuts. Pay close attention to creating a perfectly clean finish. The borders between your cuts should be almost visible. The finished ornament is shown here from several angles and under various lighting conditions.

Project Seven

This final exercise represents a stylized bloom with background leaves mounted on a small drape of material with simple stylized small knots and folds on either side. As with the other designs in this book, it is not necessary to follow the exact size of the pattern as it is presented in this exercise. You can reduce or enlarge the design to meet your own needs. The carving methodology is the same regardless of the final size of the ornament.

1 Trace or draw the pattern on the wood.

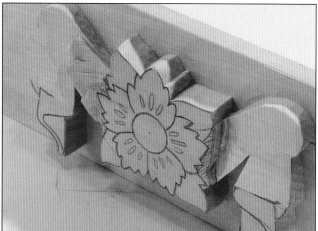

2 Outline the motif and remove the wood around the ornament until it stands free of the background. Remember, at this stage the edges of the motif should be clean with a consistent approach to cutting the outline of the motif, i.e., not on the line on some parts and only close to the line on other parts.

The outline shape must be at right angles to the background surface. When cutting the background surface, use a flat-edged gouge to minimize any edges between cuts. Remember, the background surface must be as smooth as you are able to make it at this point.

3 The top photo shows the areas of wood to be removed for the first rough cut. The bottom two photos show the results of the cuts. Notice that it is not necessary yet to cut all the way up to the petals of the flower.

The Complete Guide to

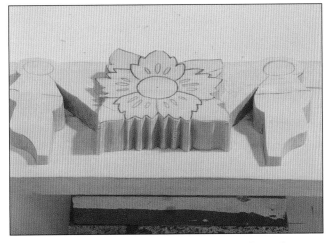

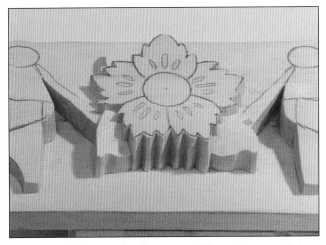

4 Carefully cut into the edges of the petals as shown in the top photo. Then mark the wood at the ends of the banners to be removed. The bottom photos show the results of the cuts.

5 Mark the wood to be removed from the tops of the leaves as shown in the top photo. The bottom two photos show the results of the cuts.

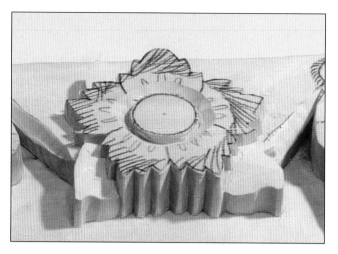

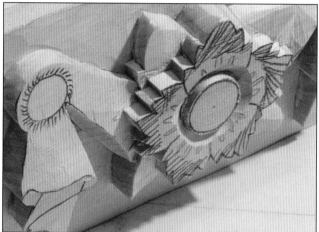

6 Mark the wood to be removed around the center of the flower and on the inside edges of the banner on both sides. The bottom two photos show the results of the cuts.

7 The next stage is to rough carve the outside edges of the bloom and the small stylized knots in the banner. Mark the wood to be removed from the bloom. Also mark the wood to be removed around the two knots at the corners of the banner.

The Complete Guide to

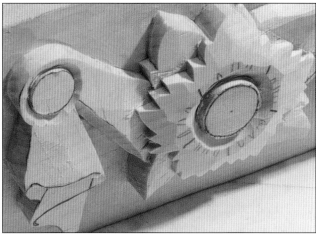

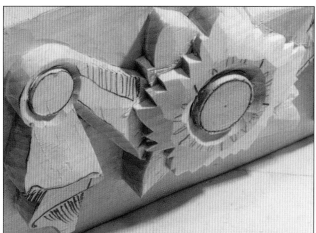

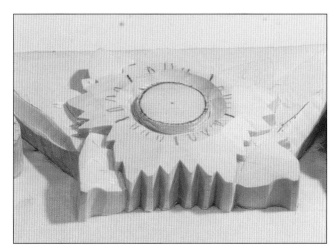

8 This series of photos shows the results of the cuts. The circular center of the bloom is now prominent.

9 Mark the wood to be removed from the banner as shown in these photos.

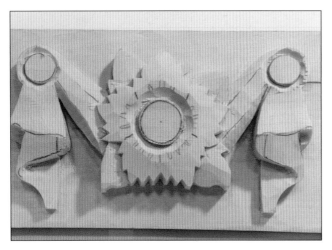

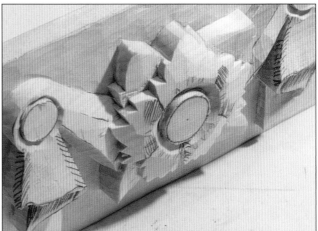

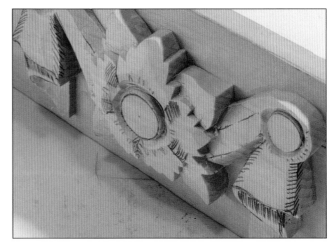

10 These photos show the results of the cuts.

11 Mark the areas where wood will be removed to add detail to the flower and movement to the drapes.

The Complete Guide to

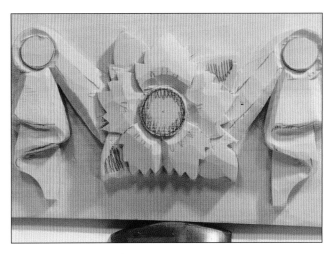

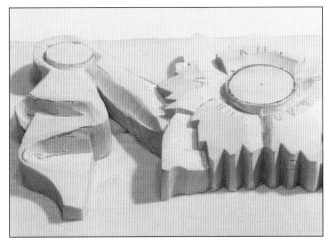

12 The series of photos shows the results of the cuts.

13 The top photo shows the wood to be removed from the center of the flower and from two of the leaves. The bottom two photos show the results of the cuts. These are the last rough carving steps to be made on this ornament.

14 Continue to polish the carving by removing smaller and smaller chips of wood from the ornament. Add details, like the veins in the leaves and the dimples in the flower petals, only after the surface of the ornament has been completely polished. These final photos are taken from a number of angles to give you an overall picture of the finished project.

As you work toward this final result, always carve carefully and systematically. Don't be tempted to take short cuts or to use tools just because they are close at hand but not really suitable for the job. Make sure you maintain the sharpness of your tools to achieve a clean cut. Good tool sharpness will help make your carving easy and much more enjoyable.

The Complete Guide to

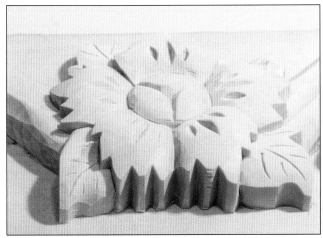

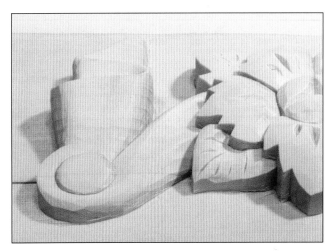

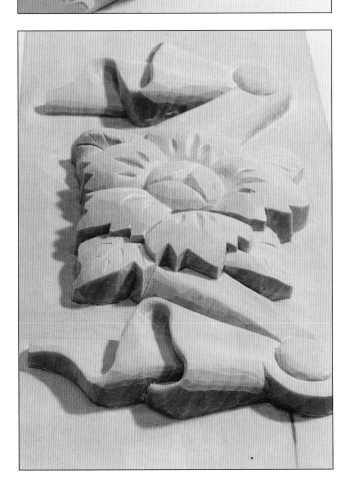

More Great Project Books from Fox Chapel Publishing

- **Architectural Patterns for Woodcarvers by Kurt Koch:** If you are looking to add architectural elements to fireplace mantles, archways, seat backs or any other item—you will not find a more comprehensive collection of patterns! From the simple to the ornate, this collection from Master carver, Kurt Koch, provides over 200 designs that can easily be transferred to wood.
  ISBN: 1-56523-194-5, 72 pages, soft cover, $24.95.

- **Carving Horse Portraits in Relief by Kurt Koch:** With over 150 color photographs, you will learn step-by-step how to lay out patterns, how to measure and mark levels, and how to create the illusion of depth by following along as the author demonstrates how to carve a horse's head in high relief. Then, apply your new-found techniques to five additional patterns.
  ISBN: 1-56523-180-5, 72 pages, soft cover, $14.95.

- **Fireplace and Mantel Ideas by John Lewman:** A practical how-to guide on building & installing the mantel of your dreams. Comprehensive, easy to read design & installation guide.
  ISBN: 1-56523-106-6, 90 pages, soft cover, $19.95.

- **Lettercarving in Wood:** A comprehensive guide to the art and craft of lettercarving. Covers essential background information on tolls, woods and working drawings; then moves forward to step-by-step demonstrations and exercises on incised and raised lettering. Includes 37 exercises and 9 projects plus 5 commonly used alphabets.
  ISBN: 1-56523-210-0, soft cover, $19.95.

- **Carving Signs by Greg Krockta and Roger Schroeder:** The woodworker's complete guide to carving, lettering and gilding signs. Includes lettering techniques and styles, full-color photographs and gallery, and a special chapter on gold leafing.
  ISBN: 1-56523-131-7, 128 pages, soft cover, $19.95.

- **Making Classic Chairs by Ron Clarkson:** A complete guide to making classic carved chairs in the Chippendale style. Features a comprehensive step-by-step technique section with easy reading text, more than 300 photographs, and a full-color art gallery.
  ISBN: 1-56523-081-7, 158 pages, soft cover, $24.95.

Call 800-457-9112 or visit us on the web at www.foxchapelpublishing.com to order!

Wood Carving ILLUSTRATED

Don't Miss A Single Issue Subscribe Today!

- **Valuable tips and time-tested techniques** from master carvers to increase your skills, save time and raise your level of confidence.

- **Clear, step-by-step project instructions,** for all skill levels, including detailed photographs and diagrams, so you can finish each project successfully.

- **Tool and wood reviews,** to help you select the right materials for each project and add detail and variety to your carving.

- **The best techniques,** including chip carving, Santa carving, power carving, whittling, wood burning and realistic painting methods.

POWER CARVING MANUAL VOLUME 3

FREE with a 2-year paid subscription!
120 Pages, 8.5 x 11 full color
$9.95 value!

Includes:
- *Complete Tool Review* • *Bit Chart*
- *Ready-to-use patterns* • *Full-color photographs & Much More!*